Single Life

VOCATIONS

Single Life
An Inside Look

Donna Kamann

Saint Mary's Press
Christian Brothers Publications
Winona, Minnesota

Genuine recycled paper with 10% post-consumer waste.
Printed with soy-based ink.

The publishing team included Shirley Kelter, development editor; Paul Grass, FSC, copy editor; Brooke Saron, production editor; Laurie Geisler, art director; cover and inside image by Digital Imagery, copyright © 2001 PhotoDisc, Inc.; manufactured by the production services department of Saint Mary's Press.

The acknowledgments continue on page 82.

Copyright © 2002 by Saint Mary's Press, 702 Terrace Heights, Winona, MN 55987-1320, www.smp.org. All rights reserved. No part of this book may be reproduced by any means without the written permission of the publisher.

Printed in the United States of America

Printing: 9 8 7 6 5 4 3 2 1

Year: 2010 09 08 07 06 05 04 03 02

ISBN 0-88489-723-0

Library of Congress Cataloging-in-Publication Data

Kamann, Donna.
    Single life: an inside look / Donna Kamann.
    p. cm.
Summary: The author discusses how she recognized God's calling for her to live as a single person and describes how this has shaped her life.
ISBN 0-88489-723-0 (pbk.)
    1. Single people—religious life. 2. Christian life—Catholic authors. [1. Single people. 2. Christian life. 3. Vocation—Christianity.] I. Title.
BX2373.S55 K36 2002
248.4'82—dc21

2001005051

*For my mother, Marietta,
who always encouraged me to tell my story.
Special thanks to Mary, Jerry, and Shirley
for their support of many of my single endeavors,
including the writing of this book.
Thanks also to Beth, Anthony, and Charlie,
and to the many people who have shared their life with me,
making it possible for these stories to come alive on paper.*

Contents

Series Foreword 9

Introduction 11

Chapter 1
A Look Back 14

Chapter 2
A Time of Discernment 20

Chapter 3
Lifestyle Choices 25

Chapter 4
Community and Family 35

Chapter 5
Friendship and Romance 45

Chapter 6
Religion and Spirituality 56

Chapter 7
Struggles 61

Chapter 8
The Gift of the Single Life 74

For Further Reading 81

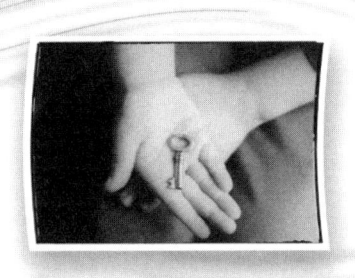

Series Foreword

An old Hasidic legend about the mysterious nature of life says that God whispers into your newly created soul all the secrets of your existence, all the divine love for you, and your unique purpose in life. Then, just as God infuses your soul into your body, an assisting angel presses your mouth shut and instructs your soul to forget its preternatural life.

You are now spending your time on earth seeking to know once again the God who created you, loves you, and assigns you a singular purpose. Raise your forefinger to feel the crease mark the angel left above your lips, and ask yourself in wonder: Who am I? How am I uniquely called to live in the world?

The authors of the five titles in this Vocations series tell how they approached these same questions as they searched for meaning and purpose in their Christian vocation, whether as a brother, a married couple, a priest, a single person, or a sister.

Christians believe that God creates a dream for each person. What is your dream in life? This is how Pope John Paul II, echoing Jeremiah 1:5, speaks of the Creator's dream and the divine origin of your vocation:

> All human beings, from their mothers' womb, belong to God who searches them and knows them, who forms them and knits them together with his own hands, who gazes on them when they are tiny shapeless embryos

and already sees in them the adults of tomorrow whose days are numbered and whose vocation is even now written in the "book of life." (*Evangelium Vitae,* no. 61)

In spite of believing that God does have your specific vocation in mind, you probably share the common human experience—the tension and the mystery—of finding out who you are and how God is personally calling you to live in this world. Although you can quickly recognize the uniqueness of your thumbprint, you will spend a lifetime deciphering the full meaning of your originality.

There is no shortage of psychological questionnaires for identifying your personality type, career path, learning style, and even a compatible mate. Although these methods can be helpful in your journey to self-discovery, they do little to illuminate the mystery in your quest. What is the best approach to knowing your vocation in life? Follow the pathway as it unfolds before you and live with the questions that arise along the way.

The stories in this Vocations series tell about life on the path of discernment and choice; they remind you that you are not alone. God is your most present and patient companion. In the "travelogues" of these authors, you will find reassurance that even when you relegate the Divine Guide to keeping ten paces behind you, or when you abandon the path entirely for a time, you cannot undo God's faithfulness to you. Each vocation story uniquely testifies to the truth that God is always at work revealing your life's purpose to you.

In these stories you will also find that other traveling companions—family, friends, and classmates—contribute to your discovery of a place in the world and call forth the person you are becoming. Their companionship along the way not only manifests God's abiding presence but reminds you to respect others for their gifts, which highlight and mirror your own.

Although each path in the Vocations series is as unique as the person who tells his or her story, these accounts remind you to be patient with the mystery of your own life, to have confidence in God's direction, and to listen to the people and events you encounter as you journey to discover your unique role in God's plan. By following your path, you too will come to see the person of tomorrow who lives in you today.

Clare vanBrandwijk

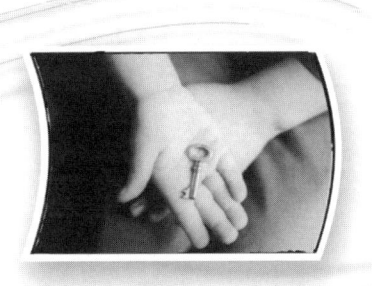

Introduction

Anthony and I are walking, taking advantage of the warm autumn day, when out of the blue he says to me, "Donna, why aren't you married?" It seems odd that after all this time, my eleven-year-old nephew has thought to question my singleness. He and his seven-year-old sister, Charlie, moved to Winona, Minnesota, with their mother when their parents divorced five years ago. We all jokingly refer to me as "the Dad" because I have been such a big part of their life. Although we are not a traditional family unit, we love and support one another, and I know I will forever be part of their memories of childhood.

I also realize that I influence the way they think. It is important that I answer Anthony's question honestly, but I also know he cannot understand my own complex thoughts about this same question: Why am I not married?

"I guess God wants me to be single right now. Just think; if I were married, I would not have as much time to be with you and Charlie." Anthony ponders a moment and adds, "Don't you want to be married?" I answer slowly, "I have always thought I want to be married, but I like being single too." With the pure confidence of childhood, Anthony replies, "I want to have a wife and some kids."

I hope to protect him from his own determination about a future he cannot possibly control. "Honey, sometimes we don't always get what we want." Anthony turns his strong, young face toward me and says, "Yeah, well, I'm going to get married when I grow up."

My name is Donna, and I am a thirty-six-year-old single woman. Writing a book about being single was not on my list of things I would do when I grew up. Even *being single* was not on my list. Listening to my nephew discuss marriage with such conviction brought back memories of my own ideas of what adult life would be like "when I grow up."

Does God call you to pick a vocation?

When do you decide how you will live? What goes into the thoughts that shape your dreams? Do you know, at eleven, what you want for the rest of your life? Do you ever know for sure? Who are the role models that affect your ideas about vocations? Does God call you to pick a vocation, or does fate decide whether you will marry, remain single, or enter religious life? Or do you just wake up one day and say, "I have decided to remain single"?

When children are young, adults quiz them, "What do you want to be when you grow up?" Before they complete high school, teenagers are expected to have some idea of the career path they are interested in as they make choices about college, vocational school, and work. Can you reasonably believe that young people at eighteen know what they want to do for the rest of their life?

Deciding on a lifestyle choice—marriage, remaining single, the religious life, or the priesthood—is daunting. I suspect that few people know with any certainty what they want from life until they have experienced different possibilities. The role models you see can lead you to believe in the option that you would prefer, but sometimes the alternatives are not what they appear to be. What may work well for one person may not fit another. The more people I listen to and the greater insight I gain, the less I think the choice is quite as simple as it looks at first glance.

When I observe married couples, I often think that they look happy and that their lives seem complete. But after meeting many married people, I can safely say that they all have their struggles. The same conclusion holds true for singles, priests, and vowed religious. All lifestyle choices involve challenges, complications, and satisfactions that may not be apparent from a distance.

I pray that you will learn what God intends you to learn.

I hope to share with you some of the joys and challenges of being a single Catholic adult. I can honestly say that when I was eleven, fifteen, and even twenty, I did not know that I would now be single or how my life would play out. When I reflect on all the factors that have influenced my choices, I am aware of a vast and complex cascade of events that shaped my life. Many situations, including my childhood experiences, have led me to the single life.

When I pray for vocations, I pray that you will be open to whatever God offers you, be it pleasant or painful. I pray that you will learn what God intends you to learn, that you will grow in ways greater than you can imagine, and that you will remain open to the unknown. You might discover your vocation in ways you never anticipated, yet you must trust that good will come from every experience you approach with love and that grace will bless your future.

Chapter 1

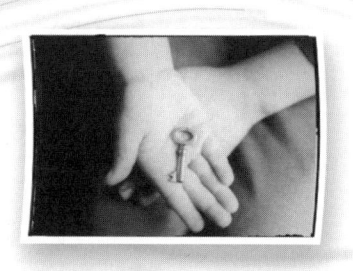

A Look Back

The summer I turned eleven, my mom was pregnant, and I was so excited. The second oldest of four children, I loved babies. Toward the end of her pregnancy, my mom set up the bassinet and filled it with the clothing she had received as shower gifts. I remember picking out my favorite, a mint-green sleeper, and holding it up, pretending that the baby was already inside.

Early one June morning, Crista was born. We children were all delighted, except Michael, who desperately wanted a little brother. He ran out of the house, crying, and slammed the door. His reaction did not dampen our spirits as my sisters and I hurried to eat breakfast and get dressed to go to the hospital with our father.

The three days my mom and the new baby spent in the hospital were wonderful days for all of us as we anticipated their return home. My father, who loved to hunt and eat wild game, had stocked the freezer with all kinds of crazy critters that my mother refused to cook or eat. While she was recovering in the hospital, he took advantage of the time to prepare his special meals for us. We all thought our father was cool, and we enjoyed these odd festive meals and his unusual presence in the kitchen.

Crista became a most coveted baby; we all wanted to hold, burp, and rock her. Hearing her crying in the middle of the night, I would wake up and go to her room. I loved holding her in the quiet of the night. She was just beautiful!

We grew up in the woods of northern Minnesota. Summers were seasons of pure freedom: running barefoot through the woods, swimming in the lake, and lying in the grass while reading. Someone had given my mother a baby carrier that we could strap on our back, so my older sister or I would put Crista in the pack and bring her with us on our adventures. We picked dandelions and rubbed them on her cheeks until she looked like a piece of sunshine, and then we brought her, sound asleep and slumped over in the baby carrier, back to my mom.

Dreams and Realities of Growing Up

Having a new baby in our family clearly confirmed what I had always known: I wanted to have children when I grew up. I would be a wonderful mom, just like my own mother. At fifteen, I outlined my goals. I planned to go to college and graduate by the age of twenty-two. I would already be dating the man I was to marry, but I would spend two years working in a wonderful job. Then we would marry, wait a year, and begin our family. I even had selected names for the children. I based this idyllic plan on my perceptions of real life, the influence of television, and my observation of others. Once I became an adult, all the pieces would fall into place, and life would be perfect.

I did go to college and receive a degree in fine arts. Before graduating, I landed the job of my dreams: working as a graphic artist in a large publishing company. Before long, I began to hate my new job, which was stressful and did not seem to be a good fit for me. I was not dating the man of my dreams either. In fact, I was not doing well in the dating department. The realization dawned on me that everything did not necessarily fall into place just because I had reached adulthood.

I decided to leave the job and start over somewhere else. The move happened quickly: I quit my work, packed up my belongings, and headed to southern Wisconsin for a fresh start and a second chance. Another two years of working in jobs I did not like and of dating men who did not begin to live up to my image of Mr. Right brought me no closer to the happiness I had expected.

How do you reconcile your hopes with reality when they do not match?

    I soon became completely disillusioned with graphic arts as a career. Advertising was dehumanizing; deadlines and demands made me crazy; sitting all day made me restless. The realization of my unhappiness hit me on my twenty-fourth birthday, the year I was supposed to get married (according to my big plan) and begin my wondrous life with a beautiful husband who loved the name Lucy for our first daughter. Instead, I was riding with a coworker in her fancy red sports car on our way to Madison for a business meeting. There I was, wearing a sleazy pink suit, pantyhose that made me squirm, and high heels I could not walk straight in. I was too many miles from home and even farther from all my hopes and dreams. I was struggling with my disappointment, anything *but* open to the unknown. My twenty-fourth year was the longest and hardest of my life.

    How do you reconcile your hopes with reality when they do not match? When you are young, you envision your future; you prepare a plan and move forward with a sense of purpose. Although visions are essential, they do not guarantee your future.

    I once had a vision of life that included marriage and motherhood. The fact that my life did not turn out this way was a terrible disappointment. The feeling hit me hardest when I turned twenty-four because that year had been such a key moment in my vision.

As you grow from your late teens into your early twenties, you begin to discover who you are, what brings you joy, and what does not work. During these years you start to sort through the realistic options that life is offering. You may be able to discern a sense of vocation as you gradually know yourself better. You may need to set aside your previous plans or to discern why life is not working out the way you had hoped. Sometimes you must go back before you can go forward.

How can I make sense of what is happening in my life?

I had to go through the same process when I faced these difficult questions: How can I make sense of what is happening in my life? Why am I so unhappy? What can I do to change?

Learning and Healing from My Wounds

In the Gospel Jesus says, "Whoever does not take up the cross and follow me is not worthy of me" (Matthew 10:38). I realize now that he is talking to me. When I was twenty-four, I needed to identify my cross in life, embrace it, and make it part of my life's journey. I needed to continue to walk with God, who loves me in spite of the cross I carry. In fact, I believe God loves me *because* of this cross.

When I was seventeen, my father left the family. My parents, who had always seemed happy to me, were getting a divorce. My mother, raised in a family where her father had controlled the decision making, learned from an early age to tend to household duties, which also was her role in our family. She did all the cooking, cleaning, and child rearing. My father took care of the finances, car, yard, and major decisions. My mother never worked outside the home and was never responsible for putting gas in the car or paying the bills.

This division of labor worked well while my parents were married. I discovered in no time at all the utter hopelessness of our family situation with my father gone. We had little money, and my mother did not have the tools she needed to function on her own.

My father drove a freight truck—a big, beastly thing with a manual shift and no power steering. The day after he left the house, I decided to drive his truck, haul freight, and earn an income.

By afternoon I was driving down a forty-mile stretch of dangerous, winding rural road after struggling to load many impossibly heavy boxes of freight. I was exhausted, trying to keep the truck on the road, when I started to cry. I was so angry at my father. How could he do this to us? Why had he not taught me how to drive this truck? Why did none of us know about the family's finances? How could he leave my mother so high and dry? I wiped my tears on my sleeve, afraid to take my hands off the steering wheel. I firmly resolved, then and there, that no one would ever do the same to me.

I thought I could set this experience aside as I continued my life. Not until I hit the wall at twenty-four did I realize that instead of identifying and carrying this cross, I had tried to bury it in the past. I honestly did not know what to do with this painful part of my history that was interfering with my life.

At the time I did not realize the wound that needed tending. Until I took care of myself, I would not be healthy enough to have a wholesome relationship. Perhaps God either was offering me time to heal or realized I was not ready for marriage, but I was still assuming that marriage would solve all my problems. The opportunity to apply this theory never arose; I am certain the result would have been disastrous.

You must take your own steps to become whole.

Many married people refer to their spouse as "my better half." Can you expect your partner to make up half of your life? Certainly, you are correct in believing that the people you love will help heal your wounds, but ultimately you must take your own steps to become whole. Finding the balance between trusting others, requesting help, and taking personal responsibility for growth is everyone's lifelong challenge, whether married, single, ordained, or in religious life.

My experience with my father left me deeply suspicious of depending on others. I wanted to marry, yet I did not want a man to take care of me. I had to do that for *myself,* along with everything else, including earning the income and caring for my home and my car. My issues with trust were not only about men. This cross—the pain from my parents' ugly breakup—was subtly controlling the decisions I made in my life.

Taking on the world by myself became quite exhausting. In my twenty-fifth year, I began to weaken, and in this frailty I was able to start reaching out to others.

Chapter 2

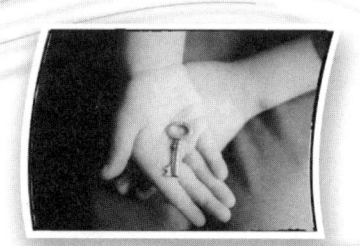

A Time of Discernment

The lessons you learn as you grow older are not always easy; the harder the lesson, the more it impacts your life. Jesus taught in parables to bring his message to people in a way they could understand. Jesus does not speak to you and me quite as directly, but he continues to find effective ways to reach you if you listen.

Life is a continuous process of discernment, but I think young adults face this process most directly. By leaving your family and childhood friends and setting out on your own, you begin to discover what sort of person you are. Advancing into adulthood in your early twenties, you question your values, beliefs, and hopes. If you like what you are seeing, you can continue in the direction you are going.

I needed deep reflection on my part and guidance from other people before I could see the light.

If you are like I was, struggling with the choices you have made, this is the time to change direction. I think Jesus helped me in his own fashion to move toward a more positive path. I needed deep reflection on my part and guidance from other people before I could see the light.

Because I was unhappy, I had surrounded myself with other unhappy people. The choices I made based on anger and discontent were seldom good ones. I had friends, but they did not share the values I wanted for my life. I was still dating, but the men I met were not good people. I was hurting myself and others, but I did not know how to begin to make amends. I wanted to ask God for help, but I was afraid I was not worth God's concern.

Lost and confused, I realized the time had come to make some hard decisions about my life. I wanted to be happy and healthy. I wanted to be able to love others. I wanted to be worthy of love.

Deciding to Be Happy

I started seeing a counselor. When I noticed the sign on her office wall that said, "God danced the day you were born," I wondered: Does God truly celebrate my life? Is God happy with me? Why then cannot I be happy?

After many hours of conversation, tears, and surrendering to my pain, I began to believe that I *could be* happy. With the help of my counselor, I reframed old ideas and realized that I had the tools to make better choices, develop healthy relationships, and take good care of myself. I also believed that God would support these efforts.

During this time I met Margie, who would become one of my dearest friends. We worked together in the art department of a printing company. Our friendship developed slowly with great effort and patience on her part. We walked every day during lunchtime, sharing pieces of our lives. My learning to trust in basic human goodness started again as I learned to trust Margie.

She was the kindest and gentlest of souls. A mentor and a friend, she shared her wisdom and accepted me into the warmth of her life. Over the years I have known her, Margie has done much to support me and help me celebrate the life I have been given. She taught me to see the gifts I could cultivate from the difficult experiences of my past. She also introduced me to a most loving, forgiving image of God—one to whom I continue to pray today.

> *Developing my relationships with a variety of people was teaching me about dignity, respect, and love.*

I gradually let go of my wounds, a lot of my old ways, and my unhappy friends. I began to understand the value of authentic friendship. Having good friends I could share my life with became more important to me than marriage. Developing my relationships with a variety of people was teaching me about dignity, respect, and love.

I now felt ready to make new choices about my career. Having never found satisfaction with the work I was doing as a graphic artist, I longed for meaningful work, something that mattered to the world. I wanted to touch the lives of others.

Making a change meant the possibility of returning to college. By this time I had been out of school five years and had managed to save a little money. I was accustomed to a steady paycheck, health insurance, and a paid vacation. Remembering my college days and the financial struggles I had experienced then, I did not relish the idea of going back to school and giving up the financial independence I had finally attained.

Day after day, I realized that I absolutely had to consider another career choice if I were to find meaning in my life. In college I had worked as an assistant in nursing homes. I loved the work and the opportunity to care for others, but at the time I had no desire to become a nurse, which I thought of as woman's work. I did not see myself in a traditional female job.

Now I allowed myself to reconsider a career in nursing. Abandoning my gender issues, I was attracted to the idea of becoming a nurse, a career that affords much human contact and ample opportunity to make a difference. I prayed about this and had long discussions with Margie. I returned to school because I recognized God's blessing in this decision.

> *One grace of being single is having more time and space to make big decisions.*

By autumn that year, I had found some peace. I believed I was on the right path with my life, and the rightness infused everything I did. School was fun; the classes were stimulating, and I was excited to be learning about health. I began taking better care of myself and nurturing my spiritual life. I became comfortable with who I am and content with taking responsibility for my own health and well-being; my life was full.

One grace of being single is having more time and space to make big decisions. I could sort through my problems, discover who I am, and return to college without affecting anyone else. Had I been a married person with children, I might have had a more difficult time sorting through my options. Parenting requires a kind of commitment that does not seem conducive to "changing my mind."

Awakening to God's Plan

I was thankful for having options and the time to discern them. During my twenties I had sometimes felt that God was not giving me what *I* wanted—for example, a husband. Now the wisdom of God's plan was unfolding before me, and I could let go of my expectations and just *be* where I was and who I was: single, alive, and growing.

For everything there is a season, and a time for every matter under heaven:
a time to be born, and a time to die;
a time to plant, and a time to pluck up what is planted;
a time to kill, and a time to heal;
a time to break down, and a time to build up;
a time to weep, and a time to laugh;
a time to mourn, and a time to dance;
a time to throw away stones, and a time to gather stones together;
a time to embrace, and a time to refrain from embracing;
a time to seek, and a time to lose;
a time to keep, and a time to throw away;
a time to tear, and a time to sew;
a time to keep silence, and a time to speak;
a time to love, and a time to hate;
a time for war, and a time for peace.

(Ecclesiastes 3:1–8)

I recognize that nothing in life is better than being happy and doing good. Moreover, for a person to eat and drink and enjoy the fruit of her or his labor is a gift from God. I recognize that whatever God does will endure forever; there is no adding to it or taking from it.

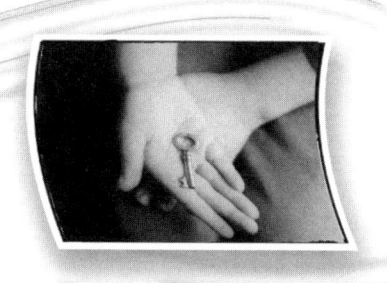

Lifestyle Choices

Everyone is born single. The tricky part about remaining single is the choice or the lack thereof. People must *choose* to be married, ordained, or in religious life, but the same is not necessarily true for single life. Single people deal with the same kinds of decisions, fears, joys, and challenges that people in the other vocations do. If you do not want to remain single, you might decide to pursue another life vocation and later be filled with resentment. You might make decisions based on the desire *not* to be single. A number of marriages probably start on the basis of this reasoning and end because of the same faulty logic.

When is the single life a *vocation*? Single life might be a vocation for those people who eventually choose a lifetime of singleness. Others who are single, while hoping to marry or to follow a call to ordination or to religious life, might think they are waiting for their real life to begin. Being single—whether freely chosen or not—can be a vocation in itself. Do you choose to be single, or does God choose for you?

I did not make a conscious choice to be single. Even now, I do not know whether I will be single for the rest of my life, but to remain true to what God has given me, I must consider as sacred this time when I am single.

Being single does not come with a set of instructions, and I cannot recommend the best way for anyone else to be single. I can only share my story and the insights I have gained. By describing my experiences and representing the voices of others who walk this path, perhaps I can help you choose what is right for your life.

Do you choose to be single, or does God choose for you?

Many of the decisions you make stem from basic life needs: a safe and nurturing home, a career that provides for you, pastimes that give you joy. Although some decisions might seem too enormous when you have not yet committed to a particular lifestyle, nobody wants to live in a state of uncertainty.

Being a single person who is not certain of the permanency of her singleness, I realize that my major life decisions require creativity from me and strong encouragement from God. I have often sensed that certain catalysts were coaxing me to move along in my decision making. When I reach a crossroad, I must make a choice.

Creating a Home

When I was twenty-seven, several months into nursing school and having considerable trouble finding a decent place to rent, I decided to buy a house. This decision was a leap in the dark because I did not know the first thing about buying a house. I continued to work part-time in graphics to have some income, but I knew that as nursing school intensified, I would eventually need to quit my job.

Early in my adult life, I learned that buying on credit is unwise. I had borrowed money for a fancy sports car that I could not afford. The initial excitement of my new car wore off as soon as the high monthly payments caught up with me. When I computed how much the car would cost, including interest, I was sick to my stomach. I sacrificed many options to pay for that car, but the enjoyment was never worth the expense.

After that experience, I learned to live within my means. I became comfortable with used and secondhand items. I minimized my expenses so I could afford to work part-time and still make ends meet. I did not know what I would do when I had to quit working, but I figured that God had gotten me this far; certainly the two of us could get me through college, one step at a time.

Buying a house seemed a bit brazen in view of these considerations, yet there I was with the Realtor, looking at a little white one-bedroom house in small-town America. Betty, the elderly woman who owned the house, was moving to a nursing home because of a decision forced on her by her family in response to her failing health and her husband's recent death. She had reluctantly put her home on the real estate market. We both felt a special connection the first time we met: I needed a loving home; she needed someone to love her home, a small and modest house that enshrined the essence of two people who had spent their final sacred years together. The house was everything I could have asked for, but I felt unprepared to make this decision by myself.

Again I came up against my expectation of having a married life. I had always assumed I would buy my first house in partnership with my husband; instead, I was on my own. This transaction was between me and Betty and God; no husband was involved. If I decided to buy this house, would I be taking a step away from married life and more definitely toward single life? Was I beginning to erase the possibility of ever being married?

I reassured myself: No, I was simply looking for a place to live! Whether single or married, I needed a home, and I was starting to sense my own nesting instinct. With the support of friends, a coworker with financial expertise, and God's grace, I made Betty an offer on her house, and she accepted. The decision felt right to me.

Over the next month, however, I slept poorly; I was excited and nervous while trying to keep track of all the tasks I had to do. In addition to work and school, organizing the many details of the house and the move required a full-time effort. When the closing date finally arrived, Margie gave me a big hug, and I left work early to go to the bank. While sitting there preparing to sign the papers, I again thought, "I wish I were married. I need someone to turn to and ask, 'Are you sure we are doing the right thing?'" When I shared this thought with the banker, we both laughed. Silently, though, I was asking God, "Are you and I doing the right thing?" I felt a resounding *Yes!*

> *I was asking God,*
> *"Are you and I doing the right thing?"*

Owning a home if you are single is a mixed bag of blessings and hard work. The division of labor is simple: no argument about who takes out the trash or whose turn it is to clean the bathroom. I do it all. To avoid being overwhelmed with the workload and the responsibility in the beginning, I reminded myself: *one thing at a time*. I have time now to do the dishes, so I will. Spending time thinking about doing the dishes every day for the rest of my life would be too much to comprehend. Worrying about what might happen when the furnace shuts down or the plumbing backs up would be torture.

Instead, I decided to cope with each day as it presented itself and to find a way to handle each crisis as it occurred. Having faith in God and in myself was critical. I appreciated the people in my life who cared for me and were willing to help. Allowing others to help me did not mean that I was dependent; we were all interconnected and shared our gifts. Owning a house became at once humbling and empowering because home ownership offered another opportunity to learn more about myself.

By owning a home, I have discovered my gifts and my weaknesses. Ideally, persons living together in marriage or community complement one another with their gifts and offset their weaknesses. Living alone challenged me to work within my own limitations. I could more easily become adept at home repairs than at shopping for basic necessities and organizing paperwork. I enjoyed the challenge of tearing into a big house project, but I hated buying milk and bread.

Living alone challenged me to work within my own limitations.

Compromise took on new meaning—not just something I did with others. Now I compromised with myself: no new house projects until I tended to basic maintenance; one grocery-shopping spree at the end of each work week, complete with a special meal for that night. By learning to keep bills and expenses to a minimum, I could live within my financial limits and avoid distasteful paperwork.

When situations were beyond my ability to manage, I sought help. With the advice of others and aided by my own perceptive skills, I found trustworthy and reliable people to hire. To feel safe, I learned to trust my intuition. If I could not talk comfortably with someone, I did not hire the person. I have found it much easier to ask for and expect honesty and respect from people in all walks of life. From fixing the car to replacing the water heater, I have discovered wonderful people who make unpleasant situations seem like a brush with God.

The Meaning of Work

As a young woman making a career choice, I never intended that my career would be a lifetime endeavor; I expected that motherhood would eventually be my primary vocation. Work was secondary and therefore unimportant. An intense distaste for the career I had chosen in graphic design drove my decision to return to school.

Because marriage and child rearing were not coming my way, I realized that I might be working for a long time. Happiness in my work became imperative. As a nurse I am now using and developing my greatest gifts. Nursing *is* my vocation, and I believe God's hand was guiding me toward this path all along. As a single person, I direct my decisions toward meeting my fundamental needs: to feel worthwhile, to love, and to be loved.

As a nurse, I am able to put my love to good use in caring for others. The years I spent in nursing school were wonderful opportunities to explore life from a health perspective. The program I attended was structured to promote individual growth and awareness of health and wellness. I learned to care not only for others but also for myself. My good health became a prerequisite for nursing others toward health.

Setting boundaries to help me stay healthy was a challenge. Many women focus on caring primarily for others. Learning to identify and maintain my own good health habits contradicted everything I had been taught. Starting fresh, I defined elements that made me feel good. I developed basic guidelines: nutritious meals, enough sleep, fresh air each day, and time set aside for prayer and silence.

After I completed the nursing program, I decided to work in moderation. Finding a balance in life seemed important, and I concluded that working full-time, tending to a house, and taking care of myself created too much of a burden. Living on student wages for four years helped me slim down my budget, so working part-time was enough to meet my income needs.

God seemed especially present to me in this area of my life.

Being a new nurse was a joy because I learned something fresh every day. For the first time in my life, I felt completely at ease in the shoes I was wearing—rubber soles instead of heels. Although I did not have much nursing experience, I felt confident I would be able to make the right decisions and say the appropriate words. God seemed especially present to me in this area of my life.

While caring for my patients, I was learning about much more than nursing. I learned about life in all its complexity. Observing, hearing, and entering the suffering of others are occasions for the pure grace of being a nurse. Seeing how loving and devoted lifetime partners tend to each other in sickness and in death taught me about relationships. Helping someone walk one, two, or three steps after a stroke had weakened his legs taught me about the strength of the human spirit. I was falling in love with humanity.

In discovering love at work, I realized that finding a husband became less important to me. God showed me how rich and simple real love is. Love is all around me, and I can reach out and partake every day.

The more you learn, the better your decisions will be if you listen carefully for God's voice.

The challenges I faced with home and career decisions are not unique to single people; everyone makes these same decisions based on personal desires, history, beliefs, circumstances, and individual gifts. These choices also involve responsibility: to yourself, your community, your family, and your God. You are fortunate to have choices, no matter how difficult they may seem at times. You also need to recognize the wrong choices, learn from them, and move on. Sometimes this requires the gentle ability to ask for and find forgiveness. No one has an accurate map of how life will unfold or is expected to pick the right path with each try.

The more you learn, the better your decisions will be if you listen carefully for God's voice. If you can also offer yourself the grace of forgiveness when you err, your woundedness will not overwhelm your desire to continue trying to do what is right, and you can remain flexible when the need arises.

Not every single person will experience several careers before finding one that fits or undergo a financial crisis before learning how to manage money. You may not want to buy a house on your own. Every situation is as individual as the person is. If you are a single person, you will have to decide what to do for a living, where to live, and how to manage your finances. Attendance at a nursing school is not necessary to learn how to take care of your own health, but this skill is a priority for you to learn. My experience may show that not much of a plan is required from the get-go, but things do work out, sometimes in spite of your best plans.

The Freedom to Embrace Opportunities

Being single may be either your lifelong vocation or a temporary state in life until you marry. My friend Jerry remained single through his twenties and used the time to grow and to share himself. He did eventually meet a wonderful woman, and they celebrated their wedding, surrounded by a community that shared their joy, knowing how right this was for the two of them.

Watching their life together change as they now become parents, I marvel at the difference in the lifestyles Jerry has experienced. I wonder whether he misses being single or regrets the time he spent as a single adult. Jerry offered me these thoughts about his experiences:

> People think of being single as being alone, but for me being single was an opportunity to meet hundreds of people I would never otherwise have encountered. I was involuntarily single throughout my twenties; I probably would have married had I met the right person. I had to wait until I was twenty-nine for marriage to happen, but those years

of being single were not wasted. Everyone I encountered contributed something to the person I am today.

During part of that time, I held low-paying jobs as a print journalist that allowed me to cover the president and the pope, makers of stained-glass windows, countless politicians and government bureaucrats, cancer survivors, the families of murder victims, people who live in boathouses on the Mississippi River, war protesters, and ordinary folks. Some people want journalists to be objective, but when you interview people about the most important parts of their life, their stories affect how you see the world and ultimately who you become.

I was also a live-in volunteer for a little more than two years at a Catholic Worker community, part of a national network of hospitality houses for homeless persons and families. The hundreds of families who stayed with us for a time, not to mention the community of volunteers I worked with, shaped who I was becoming. When I say *shaped*, I do not mean to suggest that the process was always gentle, like warm hands shaping soft clay. The overwhelming problems that people brought into the house, sometimes with anger and depression, shaped me in hard, sharp ways. But even this more difficult shaping was good and taught me to rely on the help of God and others rather than just on myself. Other people who stayed at the house gave me far more than I ever provided them. Despite their poverty, they could share themselves in a spirit of joy and teach me that what you give to others, not what you have, makes you who you are.

For six months, I lived with my grandma after her husband died; she did not want to live alone. I did this because I loved her, although it was difficult for me to move far away from family and friends and change my lifestyle to meet her needs. I was glad to be able to give something back to her after she and my grandpa had given so much to me when I was growing up.

Some people assume they will not be a complete person until they are married. I understand this feeling, but I also think about all the people who passed through my life, one way or another, while I was single and contributed to the person I am today. I would never have had the opportunity to spend time with them had I been married, and I would certainly be less complete today as a result.

People can choose to make the most out of the time they have been given, be it as a single person, a spouse, a priest, or a consecrated religious. Life provides you with a wealth of experiences at all levels if you remain open to them.

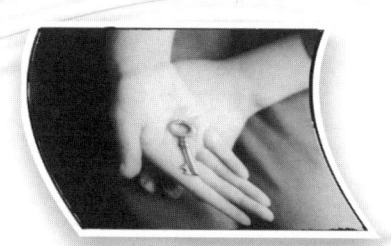

Community and Family

How to participate in community and family activities is one of the other choices single people make. Being single is not the same as being alone or without loved ones. Singles integrate their life into community as much or as little as they desire. You have heard late-night ghost stories about the spooky old man who lived alone in the little house at the end of the lane or the crazy woman who tormented small children. I am here to assure you that most single people are quite normal!

Many single people value being a strong part of community and having close family ties. Developing and cultivating these relationships is an important component in living a full life. It took me a while to recognize the value in community ties, but once I did, I embraced this welcome addition to my life.

During the years I attended nursing school, I continued living in my little house in a small rural town while I commuted to a larger city for college. After completing school, I accepted a nursing position at a large hospital in a different city. During the next two years, I spent most of my free time driving in my car from one place to another. I had developed a number of friendships in the town where I went to school, but I could not find a job there. I loved the place where I was working, but I had no desire to be part of that community. I wasn't home long enough to feel connected to the little town I lived in.

> *Having no family to give of myself,*
> *I felt called to give in other ways.*

Being part of and contributing to a larger community became important to me. Having no family to give of myself, I felt called to give in other ways. Because I was more comfortable giving time than money, I began volunteering with the church youth group, the Catholic Worker house, and a free clinic. I helped out at a summer camp for children with asthma. The volunteer work was rewarding, and I met a lot of great people, many of them single.

Still feeling a sense of emptiness, I continued to pray for a family. On 27 December, my prayers were answered as only God can answer them. My sister Beth and her two children arrived in a beat-up old Chevy and in a flurry of snow and tears after a five-hour drive across the state. Her marriage had gone desperately wrong, and she needed help.

The months that followed were bittersweet. Beth struggled with the emotional scars of her marriage and the difficulties of single parenting. The children grieved the loss of their father and were confused about their new living situation. Financial obstacles, housing issues, and health matters needed attention. Having grown accustomed to living alone for so many years and being responsible only for myself, I felt completely unprepared to welcome them into my life, which had recently been so neat and orderly. One house, one bedroom, one plate—suddenly everything changed. Three people needed my love and support, but everything felt so messy—their emotions, their pain, and the extra shoes in the living room.

One day at a time, I reminded myself. Remembering to eat, sleep, breathe, and pray, I clung to the simple rules that kept me balanced. In the midst of the messiness, I learned the beauty and resilience of small children. My sister reached deep inside and pulled out the same strength that our mother had used during her divorce. Soon they had their own apartment; Beth was working; Anthony started kindergarten, and Charlie found two-year-old camaraderie at day care.

Letting go of my individualism took a longer time. I had grown used to traveling and having my own space. I identified with a certain amount of aloneness and felt comfortable with it. The need to tell anyone where I was going or how long I would be gone never occurred to me. Having Beth and the kids with me, I did not feel as free as before. What if something happened to me? Now I had a family to worry about. I struggled with this burden, and God probably laughed—after all, I had prayed for a family!

My life took on a complex and unusual pattern. Nursing became my mainstay, the place where I felt the most focus and structure. My status was single, but now I had a family. I continued to volunteer with what was left of my free time and nurtured the friendships that had become so significant in my life.

Giving and Receiving Through Service

Volunteering more than met my desire to give. At the Catholic Worker house, I encountered a number of other single Catholics. We had our roundtable discussions at the kitchen table late in the evening, after the house guests had settled in for the night. We shared our thoughts about relationships, faith, work, and being single. We talked about living in community, working through conflicts, and loving our neighbor. We discussed important topics such as social and gender issues and other subjects as trite as hair.

I was surrounded by people I called community. Breaking bread and praying together, we nurtured body and soul. Moving beyond my basic needs, this experience was fulfilling the desires I held closest to my heart.

Still geographically removed, I continued supporting the big oil companies by driving everywhere. Although this travel was wearing on me, I was not ready to make the big decision of selling my house and relocating. In other respects I was content with my life.

In the summer of 1997, I traveled to Kentucky for a service project with a church youth group of twenty-three people, most of them under the age of eighteen. When we set out, I wondered whether I would make it. Always having ample time alone, I dreaded the thought of eating, sleeping, and working with this group.

On our first night in Kentucky, exhausted after traveling for eighteen hours straight, I crawled into my sleeping bag at 11:00 p.m. My craving for silence magnified the sounds of the people around me. Someone walked by and almost stepped on my head. Plastic crinkled; cots creaked, and someone snored while I prayed for peace.

Sometime during that trip, God did bless me with peace. I fell into a rhythm with the group and found an answer for a question I did not even know I had.

I realized the time had come to integrate myself further into community.

I remember, early one morning while walking alone in the hills of Kentucky, asking God why my womb had remained empty. God answered, "Your womb is not empty." Indeed, I recognized it was filled with my love for these teenagers, for Beth's children, for all my patients at the hospital, and for the many other people my life had touched.

When I returned home, I realized the time had come to integrate myself further into community. After all, being part of a larger group was something I could do. I did not necessarily want to continue sleeping surrounded by sixteen teenagers, but I was ready to live closer to the people I loved.

Two months later, I sold my little house and moved into the town where I now felt most at home. Work continued to require long-distance driving, but my friends and family were all within ten minutes of me. I found a bigger house with spare rooms, knowing that I needed more space for people in my home because there was more space in my heart.

Life is . . . a meaningful combination of individuality and community.

As I plunged further into the life of a single person, I could understand another layer of meaning in this vocation. Single people are not self-indulgent. Life is not a series of jobs, hobbies, and casual friendships but rather a meaningful combination of individuality and community.

While studying basic psychology in college, I read theories about how people give of themselves. Psychologists define the twenties and thirties as years for nurturing relationships and children. Once the children are gone and the relationships are well established, people in their forties, fifties, and sixties are expected to become involved in the greater community by volunteering time and talent. Older people expect that children and the community will give back to them. This is how mature and healthy people support the world around them.

Single people in their twenties and thirties are also nurturing their relationships. Although they are not raising children, they contribute in other ways to the greater good of the community. You do not have to be in your middle years to do volunteer work, nor do you need to have children to participate in the growth of children. You can choose a variety of creative ways to use your time and energy.

Serving in the Church

The Catholic church has a need and a place for the single layperson to become involved with church ministry. Single people add tremendous diversity, energy, and time to their church community. As the church experiences a shortage of priests, more types of ministry and leadership are becoming the work of laypeople. Single people have an excellent opportunity to become involved with the church alongside the members who take religious vows or join the priesthood.

You can contribute to the church by filling the role of eucharistic minister, lector, youth minister, catechist, greeter, usher, or parish council member. You can donate time and money toward fund-raisers, community meals, and gatherings. One of my friends was involved for a number of years with a contemporary choir. The group met weekly to rehearse and to share a meal. My friend became much more involved with the church community through these weekly sessions, and she also offered the gift of her lovely voice to the liturgical celebration.

My first parish had two key positions for laypersons. Marsha was the director of adult enrichment and religious formation; Jay, a single man, led music and youth ministry. These two people had a rich background in theology and church ministry. With their knowledge and experience, they offered a welcome addition to our church, and to me these laypeople seemed to be more approachable than an ordained minister might be. In one local church I attend now, the music minister and liturgist is a single woman who not only provides a vast amount of knowledge and support for these two areas but also presents a strong witness for the other single people in the parish.

I have participated in my church community by volunteering with several service trips for youth groups and by teaching religious education. A number of years ago, I participated in the RCIA (Rite of Christian Initiation of Adults) program as a candidate. A number of single people had offered their time to mentor the participants. Candidates form special bonds during this time in their spiritual growth. As a group we all benefited from one another and became close during the process.

Participation in adult formation has increased my connection to the church and helped me feel part of the larger community. Knowing an increasing number of people within the church through these connections makes me aware of the common ownership of the faith.

The Family

Family is important to most single people. Whether you are connected to your biological family or incorporate the greater community into your idea of family, nurturing a sense of family should be a priority. This family experience, as rich as it can be, may still not be enough sometimes.

As I moved into my thirties, I struggled with my desire to have children. For someone who had previously set her heart on having a family, this yearning is perhaps one of the most difficult challenges of being single. When I sat in church, surrounded by young families with wiggly children, I consoled myself with these thoughts: Kids are so disruptive; why would I want them? Doesn't that mom see those Cheerios all over the floor? Toddlers are so messy; thank goodness I am not cleaning up after them!

These thoughts did not quiet the mother in me. Adopting and parenting single-handedly did not appeal to me after I watched my sister struggle to raise her children. Having my own children would not happen while I was single.

In nursing I found an outlet for much of my nurturing side. While volunteering at the Catholic Worker house, I had the opportunity to work with many small children; endless bumps and bruises had to be kissed. Gardening also allowed me to participate in the miracle of growth.

Gifted with Family

Still I prayed to God for children. Once again, God answered my prayers differently than I had imagined when I prayed them. When I chose my second house, I carefully selected a home with plenty of windows and a large yard. My houseplants had to have lots of sunshine, and I needed space for a large garden. The house also had to be within walking distance of friends and businesses because I planned on driving less.

The house I bought met all my criteria, but it came with things I had not planned on, like neighbors with needs larger then I could imagine. A troubled family with two small boys lived in a house less then twenty feet from mine. The boys were living with their grandparents because their mother had lost legal custody of them. The many problems included poor parenting skills, lack of boundaries, and violence.

The moment I moved in, the children came: hovering around the wheels of the moving van as it backed up to the front door, waiting in the driveway when I came home from work. As soon as I opened the back door, a little head peering from behind the lilac bush greeted me with, "Hi, Donna!" When the children were not immediately underfoot, the sounds of harsh voices and thuds affronted me while heavy hands attempted to maintain order in their chaos.

Winter brought silence and a return to my privacy. I settled into my home, painting, cleaning, and repairing. I forgot about the children next door until spring. With warm air, open windows, and longer days again, I realized I had moved into more than just a home of my own.

The saying "It takes a village to raise a child" came to mind over and over as I tried a variety of methods to end the abusive situation next door. I eventually settled into being part of the village, but it took me some time to reconcile my prayers to this reality. God apparently intended me to be present in this situation that was part of my life now, and I do believe that God gives me what I ask for—even though the answer looks different than I had imagined.

So along with planting the garden and mowing the grass, my other outside tasks included tending the children next door. They needed positive words and laughter, and I wanted little faces in my life.

I am not naive enough to believe that all families have it easy or that all parenting situations are filled with perfect joy. The reality of life for everyone includes struggle, disappointment, and disillusionment. Certainly, people in traditional family settings have had to parent in ways they had not anticipated, and an abundance of small, unexpected miracles rewarded them as their children flourished. My experience has been the same with the little boys next door. Bright moments and times of healing laughter, for me as well as for them, are coupled with giant hugs and messy kisses.

> *The reality of life for everyone includes struggle, disappointment, and disillusionment.*

Anthony and Charlie, my nephew and niece, have also filled the child-shaped space in my heart. After I moved, Beth took a job working evenings, and her children began spending nights at my house. I quickly transformed the spare rooms into real bedrooms that stopped being mine. When Anthony stuck automobile stickers on the lovely old oak bedroom door, I cringed. Charlie promptly knocked over a lamp and broke the shade, and I bought glue. I insisted they learn to make the bed each morning, but the rest I let go.

Being a single adult for almost twenty years allowed me the luxury of developing my own sense of order. I could easily contain my own mess because it was quite small. I could also quickly become used to a neat house. When God calls you to open yourself to others, that openness spills into spaces once occupied by peaceful nothingness, and you have to adjust.

The children next door had expanded into my entire yard, and Anthony and Charlie had filled my house. Suddenly, *my* space no longer existed. This change disconcerted me at first, and I continue to struggle with the feelings. Sometimes I have to disappear into the woods to reclaim the quiet natural order that makes me feel balanced. At other times I am aware of the beautiful blessings that accompany these children and am grateful to have them bestowed on me. At the end of a long day, sitting on the edge of Charlie's bed as she tells me about her day, I slow down, breath deeply, and fill myself with love. The generous supply of nighttime stories and the innocent sleep are welcome additions to my soul.

Coming full circle . . . I know God has been at work within me.

When I reflect on the cross I carried from my adolescent and young-adult years, I think about how far I have come and where I am drawn to grow. Coming full circle—from cherishing a family I loved and trusted, to being able to trust no one, to learning to love and trust again—I know God has been at work within me.

Truthfully, I had feared my heart would never be open enough to give what a marriage would require. But in the last five years, I realize I have set down part of my cross: the thought that I could not love enough. When God calls me to embrace this cross now, I accept the fear, not the lack of ability. God and I both know I can love enough. What I grapple with now is my fear of that love. God teaches me in small and comforting ways to let go of the fear. God also provides ample opportunity to continue loving more deeply and with greater risk—a universal call to you and to me, whatever the vocation: single life, married life, priesthood, or consecrated religious life.

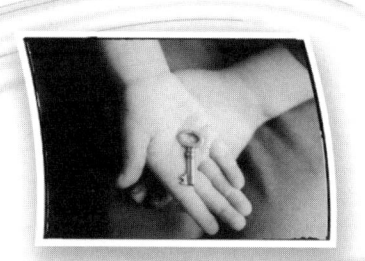

Friendship and Romance

People from all walks of life develop friendships. In marriage the spouse is also a dear friend. In a religious community of brothers or sisters, deep bonds of friendship develop and contribute to the sense of belonging. You naturally develop relationships with people who share similar experiences and values.

For me, finding single friends happened over time. Peers from high school and college had gone on to marry while I remained single. Many of the people I knew from work, church, and school were married. They were welcome additions to my life and helped me understand how to make healthy communication happen and resolve conflicts in marriage. These relationships were valuable, but I wanted friends with whom I could share experiences. I wanted companionship for the hobbies and adventures that filled my free time.

You can meet single people in a variety of ways, including church singles' groups. Of course, you can always find pockets of single people in athletic clubs, dance clubs, and social events at work. When I started volunteering at the Catholic Worker house, I made some strong connections with other single people. Over the course of time, I also developed relationships with other people who have not married.

The value of having this network of friends is beyond words. I enjoy the simple pleasure of having people share spontaneous activities like walking, canoeing, or dining out. Moreover, having people share my life is a blessing. At the end of a long day's work, I do not come home and bury my stories in a plate of spaghetti! If something is sticking with me and I need to talk about it, I call a friend. The support of friendship is priceless in daily life.

The Influence of a Friend's Life

I met Mary the first time I volunteered at the Catholic Worker house. One of the original founders of this particular community, she seemed totally committed to her single life as a volunteer. We have become friends who share many ideas, much laughter, and all our struggles.

The Catholic Worker movement originated in the 1930s with two laypeople, Dorothy Day and Peter Maurin, who felt the need to participate actively in the works of mercy and to assume responsibility for people who are less fortunate. Although the founding members of the Catholic Worker movement were Catholic and based their vision on the Gospel, they did not look to the church for public acknowledgement or financial support. Instead, they offered their time, invited homeless people into their homes, shared their food and clothing, and sacrificed what they had for others who had less. They lived in intentional communities with people who held similar values about tending to the universal needs of others.

Since inception, the Catholic Worker movement has grown throughout the United States and spread into other countries. Its basic mission is service work with a strong voice for justice. Many Catholic Worker members have spoken publicly and been jailed for their resistance to systems that neglect basic human rights and contribute to war, violence, and suffering.

Mary's commitment to the Catholic Worker movement focuses on a vision of community. By providing hospitality for homeless people, she responds to Jesus' invitation to offer a generous, listening, healing, and merciful heart to others. Although she has taken no formal vows, she has dedicated her life to this work she considers to be her vocation.

Part of Mary's vocation is being present to people in their suffering. She is a wonderful listener and has challenged herself to be a good communicator. Learning to love, to manage conflict, to resolve differences, and to compromise are among the skills necessary for living in a Catholic Worker community. Because the guests change monthly, communicating clearly and remaining flexible to the needs of others are constant challenges. The other members who make up the core community also require love and a committed relationship. Being single enables Mary to live out her vision of community and service to others, as she explains:

> My vision is based on my experience as a member of the Catholic Worker movement. My belief in community living comes from the Acts of the Apostles: "All who believed were together and had all things in common" (2:44). I have always felt that living out my Catholic Worker vocation is a concrete way of living the Christian life.
>
> I enjoy being in a house where I share meals, living space, and daily life experiences with others who are committed to the community as well as with our houseguests. Building and maintaining community mean being committed to others through awareness of their needs, gifts, and struggles. Community is an experience of love, joy, vulnerability, intimacy, humility, faith, despair, disappointment, resentment, and trust. The gift of community enables me to have deep human relationships and to experience the body of Christ.
>
> My belief in service comes from the words of Jesus, "You shall love your neighbor as yourself" (Matthew 19:19). The Catholic Worker movement has shown me who is my neighbor: the family that leaves the inner city to find a safer and more peaceful place to raise children, the family that has no place to stay because their house burned down, the evicted family that could not afford the rent, the man who cannot hold down a job because of his chemical addiction, the woman who is wounded and in need of a fresh start after a broken relationship. These are the faces of the many neighbors I am learning to love.

When I help feed the hungry, shelter the homeless, or clothe the naked, I comfort the afflicted. In serving and giving to others, I reach out to them and expand my own world to become a part of a wider community.

I have enlarged my expectations of what community offers and what it requires.

When your friends help you grow, you receive a true gift. Mary's dedication to her lifestyle helped me to look more closely at my life. I have enlarged my expectations of what community offers and what it requires. Her life has also shown me another view of what being single means: I have time to support other single people; I have more energy to help those in need; I have a responsibility to the greater community because it too is my family. The greater community may need to support me someday.

Mary has also become a wonderful friend. She often has time, as I do, for long walks in the middle of the afternoon. She is available for impromptu dinners when I want to go to a restaurant and for late-night phone calls when I am hurt or overwhelmed with someone else's pain. Over the years we have spent time developing an unconditional friendship.

Other significant relationships in my life have developed in a variety of ways and with an assortment of people. Elderly people open their homes and share their wisdom. One of my married friends always invites me to join her family for holidays and celebrations. A divorced female friend who organizes social gatherings goes out of her way to extend hospitality to me, including me in weekend ski trips, Friday evening dances, and potluck suppers. A carpenter I hired to repair a roof is a dear friend and a fountain of information when I have house repair questions. A priest I met at my former parish is a wonderful spiritual companion who shares his wealth of theological knowledge along with his love of outdoor activities and guitar music. A couple I have known since my college days remain part of my life over the miles and the years. I have watched them develop their marriage, raise their children, and buy their first house. We share many thoughts and experiences, and we support one another in housing trials and work struggles.

These are some of the people who help me feel connected and supported. I have discovered that people reach out to one another. My single lifestyle puts me in an advantageous position because I have the space to explore this wealth of human resources. All people, indeed, are the body of Christ.

Wisdom Gleaned from the Dating Scene

Dating has been a challenge for me. I have never fully succeeded in unconditional dating. My expectations for male friendships are more complicated. I remember watching, when I was a child, *The Mary Tyler Moore Show*, a television series featuring a successful single woman who lived in a beautiful apartment in a big city. Her life appeared glamorous to me because she had an enviable job and endless dates. Looking back now, I do not think her dates ever worked out well, but when I was young, she seemed to have it all together!

When I was a teenager, dating was a pleasure. I threw myself into it wholeheartedly, easily becoming consumed with the man of the moment. At fifteen, my life revolved around Tim, my first real boyfriend. I was crushed when the relationship ended. Now I cannot imagine why, but at the time the break seemed devastating. Before long, I was dating John with as much gusto as I had had for Tim. Once again, my life revolved around someone else. You can tell where this story is going: when the relationship ended, I was devastated.

After enough of these experiences, I was not so excited about dating—the fun part was over. My expectations for dating combined an unrealistic hope for marriage with an ending as painless as possible.

In the midst of all this, I knew I was affected by the ghost of my missing father and the realization that men leave. Because I found it easy to date men who would meet these feeble expectations, that is what I did. By the time I discovered my cross, I had decided that the prudent approach was to stop dating, at least until I could sort out some of my problems.

Dating can be a sacred process. In spite of pitfalls, crazy expectations, and occasional disappointments, dating is a wonderful opportunity to practice reaching out and sharing yourself with others. It took me a number of years to discover this, and dating still comes with complicated challenges, but I can now recognize the holiness in the process.

Dating can be a sacred process.

Dating is one activity in which single people can participate that excludes the other vocations. Whether you are determined to remain single forever or to keep considering marriage as an option, dating is always a choice. Spending time getting to know someone in the special way that dating involves can be a joy. Sharing yourself, listening to someone else, and learning to develop intimacy and trust are exciting aspects of dating. Dating is also a wonderful way to learn more about yourself. You can see a certain mirror image in someone else's view of you—reflections of your goodness, confidence, and fears.

Dating can also help you see your longings and your need for love. I believe God gives you these opportunities and the people you need. If you listen carefully, God also protects you from the people who will not be good for you. In prayer I came to understand the lovely people who crossed my path in romance. Some I wish would have stayed a part of my life forever, but events did not work out that way.

Be humble, too, before the great unanswered questions.
They are the infinite sea that you will never cross.
Float there; rejoice that there is always more.
When you are modified before the truth,
you are not less;
you are far more able to forgive.
> (William J. O'Malley, *Daily Prayers for Busy People*, page 104)

God calls you to experience and to attempt to understand intimate love.

There is mystery I do not understand, an infinite sea I will never cross. Each time I date, I feel I am entering into this mystery. The outcome may not always be what I would like, but each experience enriches my life in such a way that I become "far more able to forgive."

God calls you to experience and to attempt to understand intimate love. When you love intimately, you deeply and thoroughly share the person you are. You can love deeply within your family, with your friends, and with many other people who cross your path. You have a variety of ways to love as Jesus loved, and in the course of your life, you will explore different aspects of love. Some single people do as I do; they continue to date, hoping to discover romantic, intimate love one day.

Dating challenges me to understand more deeply the cross I bring from my past. What role am I comfortable with when I date? Am I able to allow myself to be vulnerable to someone else's feelings, needs, and desires? Can I share myself unconditionally, leaving room for men to come and go in my life? I am thirty-six years old as I write these words, and I am still searching for answers to these questions. This search is one process in my life that I believe keeps me reaching farther and learning deeper trust.

The twenty-first century offers a complex pattern of dating, as anyone older than thirteen is probably well aware. Television, movies, and your peers often contradict the church's guidelines for what conduct is acceptable before marriage. You hear your country's leaders speak of family values while they are publicly accused of infidelity. Sorting out all this information and making decisions that allow you to be true to your own beliefs are challenges that may seem confusing. When I was a teenager, I certainly did not completely know what I believed; my beliefs changed from day to day. Even as an adult, I find these mixed messages from church and society challenging to sift through.

Five years ago, I threw out my television, a small, black and white, secondhand set a friend had given me when I was seventeen. The picture was never clear, and I was not fond of watching, but occasionally at the end of a long day, I would turn it on just to turn off my mind. I found the programming so awful, I eventually stopped watching TV. Sitcoms and movies often presented women in ways I found offensive enough, but what these programs did to relationships horrified me. Almost every relationship seemed to start in the bedroom. People who met one day were sleeping together the next. Love was portrayed as sexual encounters, and intimacy developed between the sheets.

Nothing on the screen has changed in the last five years to uphold the image of people, of love, and of sexuality. These unwholesome images leave a strong impression on you. They contribute to the way you look at life, just as Mary Tyler Moore influenced my ideals of the single life.

By choosing not to expose myself to cheap images, I retain a stronger sense of my own value system. Learning to value both myself and the sacredness of my own sexuality helps me avoid behaving like media personalities act. Developing deep and committed relationships takes time and effort. Having sex with someone on the first date is a shortcut that does not contribute to a sustainable relationship but damages your own sense of worth.

When I reflect on my friendships, I see the value of the time I have invested in them. Trust and camaraderie, allowed to grow at a natural pace, produce lasting friendships. The growth that occurs in each friend can then contribute to the development of the relationship. Sometimes you hear divorced people say they have grown apart. I wonder whether they took the time in the beginning to grow together?

God gives you a lifetime to learn.

You will discover some things about yourself and others only in time—an abundant resource. God is not in a hurry to see you find all the answers; neither should you be. God gives you a lifetime to learn; you do not need to rush into anything. Being true to the natural unfolding of a relationship will not cause you to lose anyone God intends you to be with.

Another aspect of today's culture that I find confusing is the definition of gender roles. If you ever watch black-and-white TV programs from the 1950s, you will realize that the roles of the men and the women are quite clear. Dad works; mom manages the home. When couples date, he opens the door, and she goes in first. He pulls out the chair, and she sits. He orders, she eats, he pays. Lovely! These simple well-defined rules bear no resemblance to the dating behavior of today.

As for this particular single woman who has been opening her own doors and pulling out her own chair all her life, it is not in my nature to wait for a man to do this for me. His paying for my meal is uncomfortable enough, let alone helping me sit down! The independent part of me does not want to be taken care of by a man. Women have spent many years redefining their role as able-bodied people; I am proud of the strides they have taken.

I know men who have been hardwired to take care of women in these ways, a role they have been raised to perform. When I resist their efforts, am I rejecting their giving? Wanting to give to others is not enough; you must also learn to accept what others want to give you.

Certainly, not all men want to pay on dates, and some women like and even expect their meal or movie to be paid for. Generalizing how everyone defines his or her role is no longer possible; after all, it is not 1950 any more. But I do think that understanding your own feelings about these matters and how others react is important. Just as I want my male dates to appreciate my independence, I want to appreciate the role they prefer. Learning to communicate your preferences and treating each other with respect and kindness are the most important factors in these situations.

Another significant feature of dating is that it is seldom permanent. By nature dating is in flux: dating either develops into a deeper committed relationship or ends at a certain point. Dating requires each person to hold on loosely and often to let go completely.

Joe, a male friend of mine, tells me tales of his dating life. He loves dating. He says he just wants to have fun and spend time with other people. Joe is exceptionally good at living in the present moment, and he has had many positive experiences with dating. He has also had painful times, but he thinks it is all worth it.

> *Past experiences can become emotional scar tissue and keep you from living fully in the present.*

Dawn, another friend, began dating Dave several years ago. She told me she was frightened because she had never before felt so strongly about anyone. I envied the love she was feeling for Dave and the excitement of their new relationship. Several months later, Dave told Dawn he was interested in someone else, and their relationship came to a screeching halt. She found this experience so painful that she has not wanted to date since then. Recently, she started seeing another man, and she tells me she is not going to fall so hard this time. She is holding back because of her experience with Dave.

Past experiences can become emotional scar tissue and keep you from living fully in the present. My experiences with my father and my earlier dating adventures certainly affect the way I now approach dating. This reaction is the cross God asks me to embrace. You are who you are because of past experiences, but your life is not limited to random experiences. You are a compilation of everything you have done. To remain whole as a person, you work with your pain as well as the strength gained from even the most difficult situations.

If you allow yourself to recognize the beauty of your wholeness, you can continue to live fully. I keep dating. Dating will never have the same sense of purity as when I was a teenager but continues to infuse my life with excitement, joy, and learning.

Chapter 6

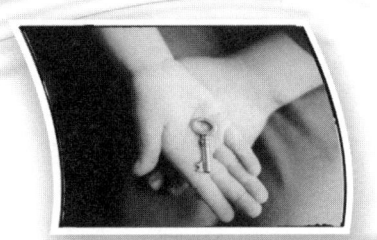

Religion and Spirituality

If your vocational call leads you to the priesthood or the consecrated religious life, you can expect a certain structure to assist your spiritual growth. If you get married and raise children, you will need to make decisions about your religious life because you want to shape the ideas your children receive. But if you choose to be single, perhaps you will have less concrete reasons propelling you to make choices about your religious and spiritual growth.

When I was exploring my independence in my early twenties, I fell out of any formal religious routine. Sleeping in on Sunday morning was easier than going to Mass. Once I started skipping the liturgical celebration every Sunday, religion gradually disappeared from my life. Several years passed before the emptiness of a godless life challenged me to re-examine my beliefs. Singleness seems to offer more looseness in this respect, in the same way that eating cold soup out of a can becomes easy. The question is: Does cold soup provide the same nourishment as a warm and well-prepared meal? Does living an empty life become all right just because I am single?

When I returned to church, seeking the presence of God in my life, I found out how much I had missed this aspect. Raised in the Catholic church and grounded in the rituals of my ancestors, I began to understand the value of religious practice. The traditions of the church are not as important as my relationship with God, but they do provide the framework for my prayer life.

Exploring and Expressing My Spirituality

No one tells me that I have to wake up early on Sunday morning, but I have learned from experience that nurturing my faith life is incredibly important to my overall well-being. Attending Mass weekly keeps me centered, gives focus to my life, and provides a foundation for the rest of my spiritual journey.

When I studied nursing, I learned about holistic health, which encompasses the physical, mental, emotional, and spiritual aspects of human life. When I care for my patients, I realize that all these areas are important to maintaining health. In my own life, I recognize an imbalance if I ignore one aspect of my health, and I believe the same process will hold true for you.

You live in the midst of a "new age" of spirituality; the media and popular culture have become aware of this basic need inherent in all people. They inundate you with all kinds of spiritual practices ranging from ancient Middle Eastern approaches to new religious forms. You can sort through all these options only with difficulty as you seek to find beliefs that will sustain you throughout your life.

The Scriptures tell me that God made a Covenant with all people and promised to be with me.

Practicing the Catholic faith has sustained me and given me an opportunity to commit to something larger than myself. The Scriptures tell me that God made a Covenant with all people and promised to be with me. I, too, have a covenant with God, the only covenant I have made in my life. Although I strive for commitment in work, family, friendships, and community, I have made no vow to anyone. My faith life is more important than everything else, and a covenant with God is in my heart.

When an acquaintance occasionally asks why I am Catholic, I explain that being committed to my faith is important to me even if I do not always agree with everything the church teaches. People will allege the wrongs the church has participated in and ask how I can accept this history. No religious or spiritual belief system is flawless. Committing to any belief includes not only recognizing that no human institution is perfect but also learning to forgive, which is perhaps the highest form of love.

You might easily move from one belief system to another while searching for the perfect one. The honeymoon phase of different discoveries has an inherent excitement and newness that energizes you, but once the newness fades, you are faced with the realities that inevitably include disappointments. All human relationships reflect this same truth. Being able to look beyond the flaws and to the potential of a person takes time, hope, commitment, and love. The reward is that you become more than just a part; you become a sum of the parts—the whole being.

I have explored various spiritual practices during my life. For eight years I studied Aikido, an Eastern martial art that cultivates a nonviolent attitude and way of life. Although nonviolence is at the heart of Jesus' teachings, I did not recognize this fact until I studied Aikido. I prayed to no god while practicing Aikido, but as I trained, I came to understand the value of Jesus' Gospel, which brought me closer to the God I pray to. Now I practice Yoga. There is no god named Yoga, but while I am tending to my body and doing the quiet, meditative poses, I am aware of God. These disciplines enhance my spiritual life, but they have not become my God, any more than has the priest who listens to my confession.

Having a committed relationship with God and a religious belief system allows you to appreciate the spiritual component in all other areas of your life. A centering point becomes even more important for a single person living a less-structured life. If you wander aimlessly from one experience to another, your life can become chaotic. The world already has enough chaos, I think.

A centering point becomes even more important for a single person living a less-structured life.

One significant challenge to single life is being committed in relationships. Married people have to commit because they must learn to live with each other even when they and their actions are not at their best. People who have taken religious vows must do the same. Imagine living in community with ten or twenty people who are all different. How challenging it must be to continue to love one another in spite of these differences! Within the church, where all members form the Body of Christ, they must love one another and practice forgiveness, over and over and over. When single people commit to their religion, they open themselves to this greatest commandment and partake more fully in life.

The following excerpt from my personal journal for May 1999 expresses my growing awareness of the spiritual dimension:

> To speak of my image of God in my life, I find myself thinking of the time before—before I knew God consciously. It was a time of great emptiness and fear: no place to fall, no place to rest, nothing inside to feel except my own smallness. I knew no stillness or peace rushing from one thing to another, one person to the next, seeking fulfillment and finding only longing. There was nothing to believe in or wish for. I tried to fill my needs externally and came up empty handed.
>
> Who is God to me now? So much. . . .
>
> Inwardly, the presence of the Spirit fills me, calms me, holds me. This is the Spirit that pours out of me into the space around me, the God that touches those I touch at work and at play. God in this sense

allows me to engage in life, in love, in caring. This God helps me walk safely through life, filled with trust for myself, my goodness, and my gifts.

Outwardly, God envelops me in the earth, the sky, the water, and the fire. This Godliness fills me when I walk in the refuge, watch birds, and pray in communion with others. When I hurt or have great need, this God comes to me in strangers who reach out, friends and family, neighbors, and coworkers.

Jesus, the male form of God, I see, feel, and hear. This man whom I can trust and pray to teaches me how to live, forgives my faults, and helps me learn the goodness and love of people. In Jesus I find my own strength and compassion and the desire to share them with others.

My faith in God has helped me to become whole. There is more to my life than I can conceive of, more than I can plan or aspire to. Trusting in God and sensing God within and around me, I am free to live fully as God intended.

At times I still stagger under the weight of my life—my concerns and anxieties—but if I remember to pull back far enough to see beyond these moments, I find the peace and rightness in God's love of me. It is so much greater than any given moment, giving me the courage to enter into the moment knowing I will come out on the other side, still warm in God's embrace, never falling into the nothingness I felt before.

Struggles

Whoever coined the phrase "The grass is always greener on the other side of the fence" said a lot that I can relate to. I often look at other people and think to myself, "They look happy all the time," or I wonder, "They seem so sure of themselves," especially when I am feeling unhappy or insecure. "Certainly, something must be wrong with me," I think.

As I grow older, I understand that the human condition is at once difficult and joyous for everyone. People everywhere struggle; everyone experiences moments of sadness, depression, and despair along with times of pleasure, excitement, and light. Looking from the outside into another person's life, you will generally see only the veneer and easily assume that the superficial first layer is the truth. "How are you?" "Fine." You are not always fine, but you also do not readily share your feelings with everyone you meet.

Sometimes Lonely

When I look from the outside into the life of others, sometimes I struggle with my own lifestyle. Walking in the evening after the sun goes down, I see families gathered around the dinner table, enjoying one another's company as they eat. Anyone walking past my house at dinnertime will see me sitting alone at the dining room table, reading. Occasionally, I am struck by how lonely this must look.

When I attend a live performance, I love to go by myself, being mindful of the performance, the music, the lighting, and the sound. During the intermission, though, I am inevitably aware of a couple sitting in front of me, leaning into each other as they share their thoughts or insights about what they have just seen. I feel left out.

One early spring day, I was taking a walk along the frozen river in a state park forest, mesmerized by the stillness and beauty around me, when a lovely young man and woman interrupted my revelry by bounding down the trail in front of me, laughing and holding hands, obviously enraptured with one another. They stopped and asked me to take their picture by the water. As they looped their arms around each other and said *cheeeese*, I wanted to cry. The peace I had just felt dissolved as I became acutely aware of their joy together and my aloneness. At times like this, I am certain that I am the only single person in the world and painfully obvious to all the happy couples.

During these moments my self-confidence takes a little plunge, and I do not feel very good. What is wrong with me, I wonder, that I am not married or part of a couple?

Last April, I was at a dance. The band was wonderful; the dance floor was spacious, and I was having a great time dancing, surrounded by friends and acquaintances from the community. Simon and Anne whirled by me, and I had to stop and admire them. When they first married, they began taking ballroom dancing lessons and eventually entered competitions. They are amazing dancers, and I always enjoy observing how gracefully they coordinate their movements. As I continued on with my solo dance, I wondered about the analogy of dancing and working together. Am I too far entrenched in the single life to coordinate with someone else?

During the next song, Anne appeared on the dance floor alone and came over to where I was dancing. She shouted above the music, "It's so much fun seeing you dance by yourself. You look so free. I don't remember the last time I danced alone." She finished dancing the song as a solo while her statement swirled around in my head.

Do all people desire what they do not have?

Do all people desire what they do not have? *Is* the grass greener on the other side? I remind myself that everyone is blessed and receiving enough, but at times I do succumb to gazing enviously over the fence.

Working Toward Interdependence

Another awkward product of my single lifestyle is an overabundance of independence. Living alone and doing for yourself over a number of years can lead to a lack of cooperation with other people. An older single woman I work with is so set in her ways that she can come across as quite offensive while working on group projects. Her strong and forceful views of how the project should be handled leave little room for the opinion of others. I worry about my own tendency to act the same way.

I have become quite adept at many tasks, mostly out of necessity. My nature is to tackle just about everything on my own, an attitude that does not always sit well with people. This approach may be effective in getting chores done in my home, but I have had to face the repercussions in my relationships and at work.

I have lived alone for the majority of my life. One year in my late twenties, I had a roommate. We shared a spacious house and enjoyed each other's company. When we began living together, we were not at all clear on the distribution of labor. Because I tended to work quickly and tore into even the biggest jobs with little hesitation, I ended up doing the majority of the work around the house. This situation frustrated me because I felt that my roommate was not doing her share. When we finally sat down to talk, she told me that I made her feel totally inadequate. She said she would be happy to do more if I were not so quick to do what needed to be done.

> *Everyone wants to believe that he or she has a worthwhile contribution to make.*

    I also recognize how harmful this independence can be on the job as employees try to work together and build trust in one another. Everyone wants to believe that he or she has a worthwhile contribution to make and deserves to be recognized. In my efficiency and impatience, I sometimes do not allow others the time to contribute their gifts to the communal work. Instead, I plow ahead, do my thing, and leave others to manage on their own. When the monthly team player nominations are made, my name is not among them.

    It is unjust for me to blame this defect on being single—many single people are wonderfully cooperative—but living in this solitary space has become a habit. My own time frame and agenda are not always open to others. When I am around families, I realize that living in a space surrounded by other people is inherently different. The focus seems to become more the common good, and tolerance for others seems higher.

    On Valentine's Day this year, I spent the morning hauling firewood with Tom, a single friend of mine. The work was hard; the day was cold, and the moment certainly was not romantic. After unloading the wood, we agreed to meet for lunch. I arrived at the coffeehouse before Tom did, and I ordered and paid for my meal because I did not want him to feel responsible for my bill. When Tom came, he went to the counter to order his food, and he bought each of us a heart-shaped sugar cookie. I had already bought a cookie for myself. I was reminded of how quickly I meet my own needs, leaving little room for others to do nice things for me.

When I was a child, I had a single aunt who was always wonderful to my siblings and me. She had endless time to take us places, and she always seemed so much younger than the rest of my adult relatives. Her spirit must have remained youthful; she was not that young in age. Now she is in her seventies, and when I go home to visit, she is still up for adventure. Emma is a good role model of the single life; we all appreciate her spontaneity and availability.

As I try to be a role model of singleness for my nieces and nephews, I hope I am presenting a positive image. I am concerned with the lack of male role models in my young nephew's life. I wonder how he will develop a sense of his masculine identity while surrounded by females. Several years ago, I tore up the kitchen to replace the sink and countertop. My sister came over one evening, and the two of us cut holes in the new counter for the sink, then hoisted the heavy cast-iron sink into the newly cut counter. While doing this, Beth and I joked that if Anthony grew up refusing to do "women's work," he would do nothing!

Although the remark seemed funny at the time, in retrospect, I wonder what he *does* think of the life I lead. Does this independence spill into other areas where the effect is not always positive? Would it be a worthwhile sacrifice to let go of some of my desire to do everything for myself so that others could come closer and offer more? Would it be better for Anthony if I hired a man to do these jobs so that he could also see a place in the home for a man?

These are all experiences I struggle with, but there are opportunities to grow, to learn to slow down, to be more patient, to increase my tolerance of others, and to let others buy the cookies. The single life will provide you plenty of room to grow.

The God-Shaped Space in Your Life

Between working, tending a home, contributing to community, raising everybody's kids, and going on endless dates, certainly there is no time for loneliness in the single life, right? Each night when I go to bed, I am alone. When I wake in the morning, the house is quiet and empty except for my presence. Going right from bed to being up to my neck in a warm bath with my eyes shut is my morning ritual. I spend many evenings in the stillness of the living room with nobody else around. I eat endless meals in silence at the kitchen table. I have come to love these moments because they are such a welcome contrast to the busy world.

When the kids spend the night at my house, mornings are quite different. My senses feel assaulted by their instant noisiness—they talk, flush toilets, and slam doors. Quiet mornings definitely resonate as more desirable in my life.

> *The question is, what brings you the most contentment?*

Not everyone enjoys spending a lot of time alone or being quiet. For some people aloneness and quiet produce an unwanted sense of loneliness. I remember my childhood visits to my grandparents, who never had a radio and seldom watched a television. Because their home seemed oppressively quiet to me, I understand how distressing too much silence can be. I also believe you can become accustomed to anything, be it living alone, living in silence, or being surrounded by people all day long. The question is, what brings you the most contentment? How do you alter your pattern to meet these needs and stretch yourself beyond your routine?

Recently, I spoke with Sue, a beautiful young woman and my classmate from nursing school. She was struggling with her career, unable to find her niche in nursing. She also shared her fear that perhaps she had chosen the wrong profession. Looking at the problem from several different angles, the two of us talked at length about some of the options that nursing offers. Finally, Sue admitted she simply was not happy and added, "Donna, this is not like me. I have always been happy!" Then with longing and sadness that I could feel, she confided that she had always wanted to marry and have a family. Now, at twenty-eight, she felt the disappointment of her present life.

The reality of her pain was not lost on me, nor could she just pray away her suffering, although I knew she was praying. Contrasting your ideal vision of togetherness with the reality of singleness easily brings on loneliness. Coming home to an empty house is difficult if you do not want to be alone.

Some single people enjoy their time alone; others do not.

Every person's life has periods of loneliness. You can be surrounded by family, children, friends, or strangers and still feel alone. Some single people enjoy their time alone; others do not. I know people whom constant companionship energizes, whereas I prefer to have quiet time alone to recharge. Living alone is easy for me because I enjoy and need this quiet time. I do feel lonely at times. If you are living alone but spending most of your time feeling lonely, perhaps the single life is not the ideal lifestyle for you.

Single people can choose to live with others, either in intentional communities or with roommates. Other opportunities include living with elderly people who have lost their spouse and want companionship or assistance with household chores and residing with single parents who exchange housing for childcare. You have plenty of creative housing solutions if you do not want to come home to an empty house. These options are not a substitute for a spouse if you want to marry, but they can meet your need for companionship.

Surrounding yourself with people is not always the best remedy when you are suffering. Understanding the source of your pain will enable you to come to a clearer solution, but the process is not always easy.

Several years ago, I attended a retreat where a presenter spoke about the "God-shaped space in your life" and how people try to fill it. This gentleman suggested that God creates a longing in you that is intended to draw you closer to God. He discussed some of the pitfalls in any attempt to ease this longing, such as substituting an addiction to alcohol, drugs, gambling, food, material goods, or sex. You can also use people and relationships in excess, hoping to satisfy your cravings.

In my lifetime I have seen people deny their pain and neglect their need for healing and forgiveness. The greater their pain, the more they try to drown it. For people struggling with alcoholism, more and more alcohol is required. If they are addicted to consumer goods, they can spend everything they make buying stuff; there is never enough to satisfy the longing. At some point they have to stop and take a look at their life, identify their pain, and come to terms with what they need.

Personally, I am most inclined to look to relationships to ease my sense of longing. At times I think having a husband would fulfill some of these needs.

Several years ago, while attending a conference in Madison, Wisconsin, I met Mark, a man I was very attracted to. We spent a great deal of time together during the conference, then continued developing a relationship from afar. We traveled great distances to be together and paid enormous phone bills. None of this mattered; I was beginning to believe that Mark was the man I wanted to marry. Never having felt this way before, I was willing to invest time in traveling, and I even considered relocating. Several months later, during a long and painful phone conversation late one evening, Mark shared some decisions that ended our relationship. I cried myself to sleep many times that night and woke up exhausted and lost the following morning.

I had promised to cook a meal that same day at the homeless shelter, and I decided it would be easier to go through those simple motions than spend more time crying alone. When I arrived at the shelter, everyone was downstairs watching a movie, so I began making the meal while Tracy Chapman sang from the radio. Two of the children who were guests at the house joined me in the kitchen, chopping vegetables and singing along with Tracy Chapman: "Give me one reason to stay here, and I will turn right back around." Before long I was laughing and singing, and the celery was flying. I could feel the pain in my heart receding, replaced by the easy joy of childhood abandon.

After the evening meal, I left to go home. Although the hour was late, I stopped at the wildlife refuge to walk and to sort out my feelings. Before I knew it, I had hiked deep into the marshland; the light was disappearing, and thunder and lightening began. I was trying to bargain with God or find a way to reverse Mark's decision when the rain came. The storm roused me from my thoughts, and I realized I was soaking wet and frightened. What was I doing wandering around in the dark in the middle of nowhere during a storm?

Walking and driving through the dark night, I clung to the thought that God would get me safely home. I realized God was traveling with my body and my spirit, which were cold, wet, scared, and tired. I started to cry again, this time with great abandon. I allowed myself to feel my pain and enter into it. Then God was with me, and none of it mattered. I knew I would get through this night. I knew the pain was all right and the rain and darkness would not be the end.

That night ended with a hot bath and a warm bed. Sleep came, and morning followed, and I was okay. With the tears, the rain, and the prayer, I had been cleansed.

Mark's presence in my life had temporarily filled the God-shaped longing in my heart—the space I want to fill with love. God was trying to help me fill that longing too but apparently in a different way. In my single life I have discovered a multitude of ways to fill this empty space. Sometimes I fill it quite purely with God. At other times I am not always able to satisfy my desire for love with a God who does not seem tangible when I long for something more concrete. Human love is an obvious alternative.

This kind of experience helps you recognize the vocation of being single. When you pray for and work at romantic love and the bottom falls out of your hope, you have to accept that God intends you to be single right now, and you must work with that choice. God continues to ask you to explore love fearlessly. Beyond fear is an abundant space to learn and grow, a space filled with God. To learn to love as God loves, you must practice; there is ample opportunity here on earth. Single people must continue to give and receive love, but they can manifest this love in many ways that do not necessarily include romance.

The challenge is to keep reaching, hoping, and learning about love.

The challenge is to keep reaching, hoping, and learning about love. This trial is part of the human condition, not something that only single people experience. People in all walks of life have to discover ways to keep hope alive. I often turn to this favorite poem by Rainer Maria Rilke that speaks to me of hope:

> God speaks to each of us as he makes us,
> then walks with us silently out of the night.
>
> These are the words we dimly hear:
>
> You, sent out beyond your recall,
> go to the limits of your longing.
> Embody me.
>
> Flare up like flame
> and make big shadows I can move in.
>
> Let everything happen to you: beauty and terror.
> Just keep going. No feeling is final.
> Don't let yourself lose me.

Nearby is the country they call life.
You will know it by its seriousness.

Give me your hand.

(*Rilke's Book of Hours: Love Poems to God*, page 88)

When I read Rilke's image that God "walks with us silently out of the night," I am reminded of the night in my life, the darkness that haunted me in my twenties, and the cross from my past. I believe I will have in my lifetime all the help I need to heal from any darkness, all the strength for whatever cross. God is with me in my fear of abandonment. As the stages of my life unfold, I will continue to trust in this presence. God is the space wherein I am challenged to unravel the mystery and recognize the gift of being single.

Called to Love

Mike is a twenty-two-year-old single man who recently moved into my neighborhood after graduating from college. He lives in an intentional community, doing service work and contributing to the lives of others in need, and is active in social-justice ministry. Rather then hauling wood on that Valentine's Day with Tom and me, he spent time writing down some thoughts on the single life:

> The dog, Buddy, cannot be left alone. He follows a human—any human—everywhere. If he is left even for a few minutes, he begins to cry and whine. Where did he learn this behavior? Is it some canine neurosis he picked up from a troubled litter, or is it learned, taught to him by someone, maybe by me?
>
> At certain times I feel the same as our pooch. They are the sad times, the dark moments, usually in the minutes before I fall asleep. An empty bed and cold covers are reminders of my singleness. The sense of being abandoned for an eternity, unloved and unlovable, is a heavy weight, a sinking sensation that fails to lull my sleeping body. Rather, I drop like a stone into the cold, watery depths of despondency.
>
> I ache, yearning for another to complete me. Somewhere inside me is a wound, an open and tender space that searches for the other,

the missing half. Consciously, I know this romantic myth is as truthful as the tooth fairy; no soul mate waits for anyone. True love is not found at first sight; it is hard work. I grow to love the other as I grow to love myself. Yet, today's culture holds out the illusion of easy love for me to buy.

We are sinful creatures full of disappointments, weaknesses, and wounds. Our relationships are inherently broken ones, always in need of more work. But when we fail to commit to that work, when we continue to dwell in a media-constructed illusion of a perfect mate, we reject reality and instead reach for a nonexistent ideal. We turn our back on the real person, dismissing what is imperfect, what is human.

Every time I do this, I am rejecting not just what is human but what is divine. God desires people to live in right relationship with one another, to work at love. When we dismiss the other for imperfections, for failure to be the ideal, we dismiss what is divine in the other. In our steadfast quest to fill the empty ache that exists inside, we deny the real source for the quenching, a complete giving over to Christ, the ultimate bride or groom.

Mike touches on the basic longing with which single people must grapple in the process of coming to understand God's challenge to love and grow. Ultimately, all are called to love.

During the Lenten season, I read Henri Nouwen's *In the Name of Jesus*, in which he speaks of God's divine love and our human reflection of it:

> Knowing God's heart means consistently, radically, and very concretely to announce and reveal that God is love and only love, and that every time fear, isolation, or despair begin to invade the human soul this is not something that comes from God. This sounds very simple and maybe even trite, but very few people know that they are loved without any conditions or limits. This unconditional and unlimited love is what the evangelist John calls God's first love. "Let us love," he says, "because God loved us first" (1 John 4:19). The love that often leaves us doubtful, frustrated, angry, and resentful is the second love, that is to say, the affirmation, affection, sympathy, encouragement, and sup-

port that we receive from our parents, teachers, spouses, and friends. We all know how limited, broken, and very fragile that love is. Behind the many expressions of this second love there is always the chance of rejection, withdrawal, punishment, blackmail, violence, and even hatred. . . . These are all the shadow side of the second love and reveal the darkness that never completely leaves the human heart.

The radical good news is that the second love is only a broken reflection of the first love and that the first love is offered to us by a God in whom there are no shadows. Jesus' heart is the incarnation of the shadow-free first love of God. From his heart flow streams of living water. He cries out in a loud voice, "Let anyone who is thirsty come to me! Let anyone who believes in me come and drink" (John 8:37). "Come to me, all you who labor and are overburdened, and I will give you rest. Shoulder my yoke and learn from me for I am gentle and humble in heart and you will find rest for your souls" (Matthew 11:28, 29). (Pages 25–27)

Yearning for love in my life and struggling with my loneliness and God-shaped emptiness, I take heart in these reflections that encourage me to accept the goodness of human love and to fill my deeper need for love with God. The single life includes the grace to have strong images of love to summon when I am consumed with the loneliness and despair that occasionally touch everyone.

Chapter 8

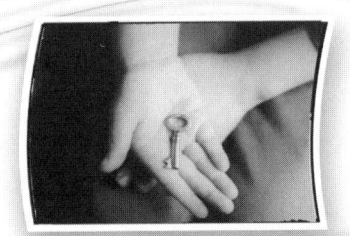

The Gift of the Single Life

Ken, a man I met recently, told me he is single because his vocation requires all his attention and energy. No, he is not a priest or a brother! Ken is dedicated to working for the welfare of others and has spent his adult life doing service work. There were times in his younger years when he contemplated marriage, but upon reflection he is glad he has not married. Now in his late thirties, he has discovered that being single allows him to live out his vision of life.

As we discussed the merits of being single, Ken sat in the rocker with a large loom in his lap, hands busily quilting an intricate wall hanging. He had spent the last three years working with the poor in the Appalachian Mountains of Kentucky. There the local women taught him to quilt. In that same community, he learned to make a mean kettle of soup and to repair just about anything broken in the house. I cannot help but be amazed at the variety of skills his lifestyle has enabled him to learn.

One gift I recognize in my life is the jack-of-all-trades I have become. Living independently teaches a person to be competent at a variety of tasks; the opportunities are fun and challenging. When I occasionally go over my head in a new project, I experience a certain adrenaline high and sing the opening line of an old commercial, "I can bring home the bacon, fry it up in a pan" and ad-lib new verses to complete the jingle. Variety *is* the spice of life!

*Living independently
teaches a person to be competent
at a variety of tasks.*

Being single also allows for an enormous amount of freedom to explore life without worrying about prior commitments to a partner, children, or community. Not that you cannot be committed to people and projects, but the commitment is different than for those who have taken vows.

Being single also offers you continual insight into your personal cross, your struggles and fears. Single life has offered me the time to sort through my childhood experiences as well as my beliefs, values, passions, and emotional scars. I have more time for *me*, valuable time to look carefully at life's lessons and to find the positive outcomes. My life has more space for people, the great variety of people who have helped me grow and those I have helped. This dense network of human connections brings me closer to God.

Moments to Celebrate

How do you celebrate the single life and recognize the gifts it holds? What are the rituals? Married life begins with a festive celebration, called a wedding, followed by yearly anniversaries. Married couples exchange gifts and set aside special time to celebrate their marriage. People who have taken religious vows also recognize the importance of celebration and ritual to mark the milestones of their vocation.

No universally recognized event celebrates the single life. Nobody has ever had a "shower" for me. When I set up my first home, I bought my own potato peeler, mixer, and cookie sheets. I have contributed to more wedding and baby gifts than I can imagine, enough to supply my kitchen with new equipment twice over, yet I eat off secondhand plates because they fit my budget eighteen years ago!

Last year, when my youngest sister married, I bought the new silverware she had listed in the gift registry, not without complaining to my other sister, Beth, "Why am I buying her new silverware when I do not even have six forks that match?" That year, for my birthday, Beth suggested I register somewhere for silverware, and she purchased the gift for me. This past year, Beth registered for an extension ladder, and I gave it to her as a birthday present. At this rate, over the next twenty years I expect to have one complete shower!

Although formal events may be few and far between, plenty of important rituals celebrate the single life. They include the simple things you do from day to day and the seasonal ways you mark the passage of time, relationships, and successes.

The entire year is filled with opportunities to celebrate and participate in life.

Each winter, a group of my single friends gathers for a progressive dinner, going to each house, eating one course at each place. We enjoy good food, lively conversation, and a break from the cold winter. Also in winter, I go cross-country skiing alone at least once. Coming down the trail through a run of white pines during a light snowfall is pure bliss and gives me abundant cause to be thankful for the single life that allows me such freedom.

In the spring, as soon as the snow begins to melt, I pack fruit and a thermos of tea for a hike to the top of Perrot Ridge, where the first pasqueflowers bloom on the rocky bluff. The occasion celebrates rebirth, time alone with God, and my single life.

In April, our community has an annual fund-raising gala, a semi-formal dance. All the single women gather prior to the event to exchange dresses. The past three years, I have found lovely prom-style dresses at the secondhand store. We all get dressed in our finery, go to a pre-gala gathering, eat fancy finger food, and then attend the dance. Men who usually wear blue jeans dress in a tuxedo, and we all gather on the dance floor. The event is a wonderful way to end the winter blues, and I look forward to it every year.

As soon as the ice on the river breaks up, I set aside time for a solo kayak trip. I never invite anyone to join me; a companion would distract me from the pure satisfaction of being on the fresh blue water, surrounded by chunks of ice, with birds flying overhead and the smell of spring in the air.

In the summer, group gardening projects and flower exchanges bring my friends together to share stories and fresh produce. Late in July one year, I was at Mary's when her single friend, John, arrived from Oregon. Because someone had just delivered a pile of fresh beets and tomatoes, we all started cleaning the vegetables and talking. Soon we had created a beautiful meal together. Much to my pleasure, some single men have taken advantage of their singleness and have learned to cook extravagantly well!

Autumn brings the annual trip to the apple orchard, long walks, and the return of wool sweaters. The children go back to school, and I take advantage of this opportunity to swing in the empty park! When my birthday arrives in September, my friends celebrate with a barbeque in my backyard pit. The group resembles any other family gathering, complete with abundant food, children, and song.

Soon December arrives, and with my friends I head to the tree farm for the annual Christmas tree cutting party. I decorate my tree alone in the evening, enjoying the contrast between that day's joyous group and the sacred space I create in my own home for the season.

The entire year is filled with opportunities to celebrate and participate in life. As a creature of habit, I have developed wonderful repetitive rituals that make the seasons special. Whether you create your own rituals or remain flexible at each moment, being single offers you a great range of opportunities for celebration.

Freedom of choice

Another gift of single life is *choice*. Although some choices are difficult and at times overwhelming, I am grateful for the variety of choices my life offers. Many people have little in the way of choice as they struggle with financial constraints, the needs of their family, and a demanding job. Being single allows me to travel lighter by living in a small house, making less money, and driving a small car. I am grateful for this simplicity.

Emotionally, I sense an abundant well of resources. Being single has allowed me to live out my vision of nursing. Spending the entire day with people who are ill or suffering is challenging. Coming from my quiet home and fresh from sleep, I can usually be fully present to my patients. Nurses who have been up half the night with their small children do not have this advantage.

During my shift I may work late into the evening sitting beside the bed of someone who is dying, helping a weak patient eat, administering medications, or treating wounds. One cold winter afternoon, I was discharging a patient from the hospital after a bad car accident. While we were waiting in the lobby for his wife to bring the car, he shared with me how poor his luck had been. Just then, his wife came in and told us that the car would not start; the battery was dead. I arranged for a maintenance person to bring another car and jumper cables to the driveway, and we were able to get the car started. Standing outside in the cold evening, holding the jumper cables in one hand, and supporting the patient with the other, I was aware of the strength my single life gives me. I have learned not only to start a car but also to give one hundred percent at work without cheating anyone waiting at home.

Sometimes after a long day, I go home and collapse on the couch, lie under my favorite comforter, and sleep until I am refreshed again. Naps are one of the true pleasures of the single life that I cannot imagine living without!

My life has been filled with joy. All single people probably do not feel that way, but many do. If I never marry, I will still feel that my life has been full.

Several years ago in the spring, I was backpacking on an island in Lake Superior. The weight of my backpack forced me to watch my footing carefully as I hiked the narrow, rugged paths. Signs of spring were all around me; flowers were budding, and the groundcover poked through. Ferns were in various stages of unfolding, some curled tightly into balls, others just beginning to leaf out, and some fully open. These ferns seemed to represent the stages of life, and I wondered where I was in my life: still curled tightly or just partially open? No, I thought; I am fully open now.

This new realization struck me. I was no longer a child or even a young adult. Somehow I had grown up. As a child I always thought parents were grown up. When I entered my twenties and had no children, I refused to claim adulthood. I would remain young until I married and had a family. But now, here I was, an adult.

> *The gifts that come with being single have taught me much about love and compassion.*

There is not a minute of this life I would exchange. The gifts that come with being single have taught me much about love and compassion. The pain I experienced has helped me care for others in their suffering. The joy I felt has filled me with hope and the desire to rise each new day. The many people who graced my life have left something of themselves, making me stronger, wiser, and happier. Living the single life has been a most bountiful and beautiful way to exist.

On the last leg of a trip to Ohio, in the evening hours after a layover in Chicago, I boarded the train. The young man sitting next to me was traveling from Mexico, heading to Elkhart, Indiana, for the auto races. He was so excited showing me pictures of his favorite cars and telling me stories of his life in Mexico. He pulled out his wallet and showed me photos of his family and his girlfriend. Then he inquired, "What about you? Are you married?" By this time I had settled in for the night, curled in the seat and covered with a blanket. Comfortable and sleepy, I answered simply, "No, I am not married." The young man looked surprised and immediately asked, "Why not?" I gave him the short, easy answer by replying, "Oh, I don't know. I guess I have not met the right person yet."

As I drifted off to sleep with the gentle rocking of the train, I too wondered why I was not married. Because I later took the time to reflect more deeply on this question and to write this book, I was able to share with you the *long* answer.

I hope that as you live your life fully, you will remain open to the questions, trust in the mystery, and be present to and celebrate the vocation God blesses you with.

For Further Reading

Coombs, Maria Theresa, and Francis Kelly Nemeck. *Discerning Vocations to Marriage, Celibacy, and Singlehood*. Collegeville, MN: Liturgical Press, 1994.

Nouwen, Henri J. M. *Intimacy*. San Francisco: Harper, 1998.

Palmer, Parker J. *Let Your Life Speak: Listening for the Voice of Vocation*. San Francisco: Jossey-Bass, 2000.

Acknowledgments *(continued from page 4)*

The scriptural quotations contained herein are from the New Revised Standard Version of the Bible: Catholic Edition. Copyright © 1993 and 1989 by the Division of Christian Education of the National Council of the Churches of Christ in the United States of America. Used by permission. All rights reserved.

The quote on page 51 is from *Daily Prayers for Busy People,* by William J. O'Malley (Winona, MN: Saint Mary's Press, 1990), page 104. Copyright © 1990 by Saint Mary's Press. All rights reserved.

The quote on pages 70–71, "Gott spricht zu jedem . . . God speaks to us," is from *Rilke's Book of Hours: Love Poems to God*, by Rainer Maria Rilke, translated by Anita Barrows and Joanna Macy (New York: Riverhead Books, 1996), page 88. Copyright © 1996 by Anita Barrows and Joanna Macy. Used with permission of Riverhead Books, a division of Penguin Putnam.

The quote on pages 72–73 is from *In the Name of Jesus: Reflections on Christian Leadership*, by Henri J. M. Nouwen (New York: Crossroad, 1989), pages 25–27. Copyright © 1989 by Henri J. M. Nouwen. Used with permission of Crossroad Publishing Company, New York.